Women Behind Bars

by Raymond G. Wojda and Judy Rowse
Photos by Grace L. Wojda

ACA
FOUNDED 1870

ACA Staff:

Reginald A. Wilkinson, President
James A. Gondles, Jr., Executive Director
Gabriella M. Daley, Director, Communications and Publications
Leslie A. Maxam, Assistant Director
Alice Fins, Publications Managing Editor
Michael Kelly, Associate Editor
Mike Selby, Production Editor

Special thanks to Joyce McGinnis for her help.

Printed in the United States by Edwards Brothers, Inc., Ann Arbor, Michigan

ISBN 1-56991-049-9

This publication may be ordered from:

American Correctional Association
4380 Forbes Boulevard
Lanham, MD 20706-4322
1-800-ACA-JOIN

Library of Congress Cataloging-in-Publications Data

Wojda, Raymond G.
    Women behind bars / by Raymond G. Wojda and Judy
  Rowse ; photos by Grace L. Wojda.
      p. cm.
    ISBN 1-56991-049-9 (pbk.)
     1. Women prisoners—Ohio—Marysville—Case studies. 2. Women prisoners—Ohio—Marysville—Pictorial works. 3. Ohio Reformatory for
  Women.   I. Rowse, Judy.   II. Title.
  HV9481.M3720358   1996
  365'.6'082—dc20
96-25770
CIP

This one's for Mary Cross.

Table of Contents

Preface

There are more than 50,000 women incarcerated in state or federal prisons in the United States. We believe that it is important for those in corrections to know something about this growing population. *Women Behind Bars* provides an important and insightful look into the lives of some of these women and the correctional officers and administrators charged with their care.

These vivid words and pictures depict a group of people whose lives are as varied as those in society and who cope with their incarceration in different ways. The inmates reveal hope, frustration, stubbornness, pride, and resignation through stories that are candid and sometimes shocking. However, this book does not give only "their side." The observations and reflections of correctional staff are included, and this makes *Women Behind Bars* a balanced, firsthand account of life inside a prison for women.

People in the field of corrections know that their work can be frustrating. Some programs work, others do not, and there is no one-size-fits-all approach that will rehabilitate all offenders. This book illustrates that point. The reader is introduced to inmates with multiple convictions as well as first-time offenders. Among these inmates are those who tend to make trouble and those who just want to do their time and get out. Yet, this book also shows that there are inmates who are truly interested in learning practical skills and pursuing an education during their incarceration.

Correctional staff should be proud that there are women in prison who, in their own words, are expressing such interest in their own rehabilitation. This is summed up by one of the inmates in this book who says, "I feel like when I leave here, I'm going to be somebody."

James A. Gondles, Jr.
Executive Director
American Correctional Association

Introduction

After the publication of our book on a men's close security prison, *Behind Bars*, we decided to try to do the same thing with a women's prison. Yet, the initial visits were unfullfilling. Unlike the men, the women did not have stories about weapons, knifings, rapes, and beatings.

The overall atmosphere was different, too. The tension that one feels in a men's facility was noticeably lacking. The officers at Marysville do not carry PR-24s (commonly called billy clubs), and the rules seemed a lot less strict. In short, a book about life in a women's prison was beginning to look a bit boring. Then, we started the interviews. The population explosion that is taking place in our women's prisons is overwhelming. Mandatory sentencing laws are confining more women for longer periods of time. The drug culture is putting more—and younger—women behind bars. Unlike most of the men we had interviewed, many of these women were first-timers who, as one administrator put it, "had an obstacle, removed it, and make model prisoners."

Most of the women have children on the outside. Many of them are single and have had their children taken away from them. Those who enter prison pregnant see their babies for only a few days before they are separated.

In the process of interviewing and photographing the women of Marysville, we began to see different classifications of inmates, and markedly different approaches to women "doing their time."

Increasingly, we realized that when most people think of a prison inmate, they automatically think of men. They do not think in terms of mothers and grandmothers serving time.

We have chosen to tell these stories through the eyes of those who spend their days at the prison. After setting the stage, we have allowed both the inmates and the officers to tell their own stories, to make their own observations, and to be as forthright as they choose.

To prevent retaliation among inmates, and to protect the identities of the innocent, we changed all the names. We also have changed the names of all geographical locations where the crimes were committed or where the inmates lived before coming to Marysville.

Raymond G. Wojda
Judy Rowse
Grace L. Wojda

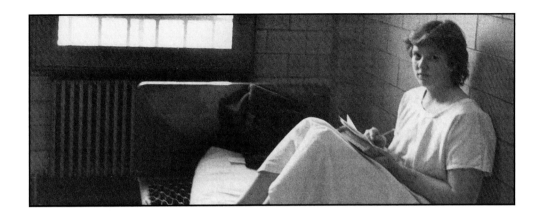

"I really don't want them to see me here."

1

Marysville, Ohio probably is known best as the home of a Honda automobile plant. However, the rural community northeast of Columbus is also home to another fast-growing industry: the Ohio Reformatory for Women.

From a distance, the Ohio Reformatory for Women easily could pass for a college campus. Located at the edge of town, where the alfalfa and corn fields meet the city limits, the reformatory is a collection of the twenty brick and stone buildings just like many others in that part of the Midwest. For most of its history, the analogy between the reformatory and a college campus was a fair one.

YARD WORK. *An inmate mows the lawn outside the administrative building. All inmates are required to work.*

The reformatory had no fences, and few of its prisoners were considered dangerous. Twenty years ago, the population was a mere 257 inmates.

Today, tall fences topped with razor wire surround the 260-acre complex, and the inmate population has mushroomed to more than 1,700. Although women account for only 6 percent of the prison inmates in the state of Ohio, their numbers are growing at an alarming rate. While the number of men behind bars has tripled over the past two decades, the number of incarcerated women has grown more than sixfold.

GRACIE. *The elderly sometimes are incarcerated. She will probably spend her remaining days behind bars.*

"I really don't want them to see me here."

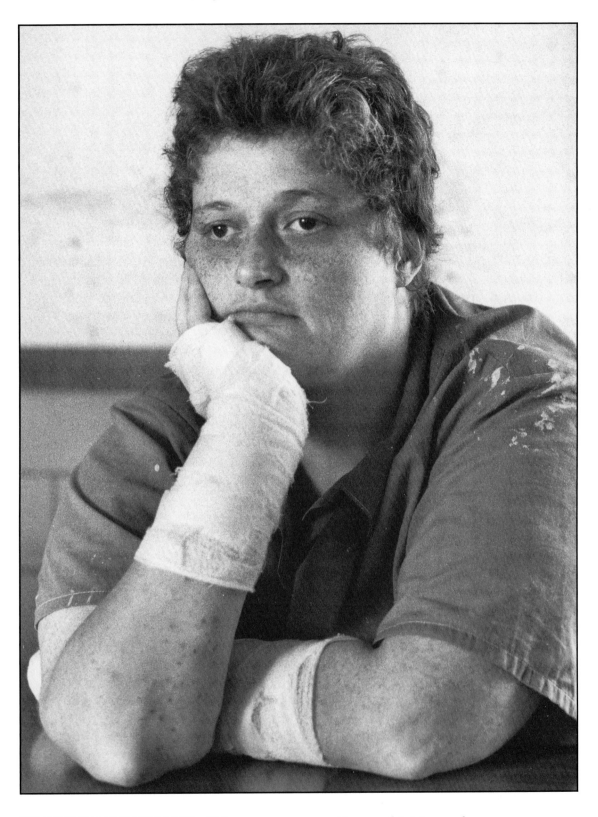

WOMAN WITH BANDAGES. *This woman was on the psychiatric ward.*

Much of the increase is drug-related. Nationally, nearly a third of women prisoners are locked up because of drug-related offenses. At Marysville, approximately one-half of the women are incarcerated specifically for drug-related offenses, and many more admit to being under the influence of drugs or dependent on drugs at the time of their crime.

The women of Marysville are mostly first-time offenders (73 percent), and most are less than forty years of age. However, there are a number of older women. Sixty percent of the inmates are African American; 40 percent are white. According to the American Correctional Association, the national distribution is somewhat different: 49 percent African American; 48 percent white or Hispanic.

The crimes of the women of Marysville range from passing bad checks to murder. A recent case-by-case review showed that 10 percent of the women had documented evidence of domestic violence against them leading to their specific crime. Countless others claim a history of such violence.

CLASSIFICATION

The prison houses inmates with all types of security classifications. Classification is the process by which an inmate is assigned a security level. In general, this process considers the inmate's offense and criminal history, institutional behavior, any psychological or health problems she may have, family history, employment history, and other factors. Each inmate is classified shortly after admission, and reclassification hearings are held at regular intervals throughout her sentence.

With good behavior, satisfactory performance in her work or school assignment, and some effort to participate in self-help or treatment programming, most inmates can achieve and maintain minimum custody. Minimum custody offers the inmate the highest degree of personal freedom in the institution, and some additional privileges (such as more phone calls, longer visits, a wider range of work assignments, and other benefits). At Marysville, half of the women are classified as minimum security, while medium-security prisoners (35 percent) make up the second largest category. Rounding out the population are close-security (11 percent) and maximum-security inmates (4 percent). In addition, the facility houses an honor camp that comprises about 12 percent of the population.

Classification determines how much time an inmate can spend out of her room or cell and where she lives. Living conditions range from single cells to cottage-style housing to open dormitories, depending on classification. Women of different classifications are not permitted to mix with each other except during work assignments.

A different color blouse is assigned for each custody level, so staff can immediately identify inmates in each group. Maximum-custody inmates wear orange blouses; close custody, blue; medium security, pink; and minimum security, green. All inmates wear khaki slacks or skirts. The women must wear institutional uniforms until 4:00 P.M. every day. At other times, they may wear their own clothing and limited personal jewelry. The inmates are allowed to receive one package or box per quarter and two food boxes per year. Among the items defined as "contraband," or forbidden, are pens, pencils, Polaroid photographs, glue, lipstick or any other cosmetic in a metal case, toothpaste, and cash.

ECONOMICS

While the inmates are provided with clothing, toiletries, and food, most choose to spend money in the facility commissary, which sells some food items, toiletries, cosmetics, and cigarettes. Inmates may receive money from their families and are required to have a paying work or study assignment in the institution. Institutional pay ranges from $18 to $90 per month. All income is deposited directly into the inmate's account; all purchases are deducted directly from that account. Cash is forbidden, so the inmates have developed an economy in which clothing, commissary items, and services (such as ironing) are used as currency.

Throughout most of this country's history, conventional wisdom has held that "Men commit crimes of greed, and women commit crimes of need." For every Dillinger, hundreds of women were serving time for adultery or prostitution. For every Capone, countless women had turned to crime because social and economic circumstances had left them stranded. The Belle Stars and the Bonnie Parkers stand out in our memories precisely because they were rare. When we think in terms of career criminals, master thieves, or psychopathic killers, such names as Lucky Luciano, Willie Sutton, or Jeffrey Dahmer immediately come to mind, but we are hard pressed to come up with their female counterparts. Indeed, Lizzie Borden is remembered not so much because of her heinous crime, but because it was a woman who committed the crime.

However, the times are changing. Although economic need still seems to be the largest common denominator among the

DISCIPLINARY CONTROL CELL: *Inmates who have violated serious prison rules are put in isolation.*

female inmates, increasingly we are witnessing a different pattern. Women with extensive histories of criminal activity—fed by the increase in the drug culture—are becoming almost as commonplace as men.

JANET

Janet is in the first year of a seven to twenty-five-year sentence for killing her husband during an argument. Currently, she is a maximum-security inmate. She is in her late thirties, with blonde hair growing out of a short cut.

"I had to keep my hair short, and he didn't like me with makeup on. If he changed his mind, it was only to allow eye shadow. He didn't want me attracting somebody else.

"He was very manipulative. I was very much in a prison. I was under watch all the time. I have more freedom here than I had in my own marriage. It was a very abusive marriage. I couldn't get real dressed up, unless it was for work. But he even checked on me at work. I had to watch how I acted, how I dressed. I was raising the children his way. How I was raised was a totally different way, but I had to go along with everything he said.

"I tried to leave, but I always went back. I didn't think I had any place to go. He was always out there hunting me down. And I couldn't tell anybody. When you're in a situation with that much stress, you get paranoid. Where is he now? Am I going to do anything today to get hit?

"I'm in a battered woman's group. There are women in here not what I'm here for, but they've been through what I've been through, so they understand. I was ashamed at first, and I didn't talk about it a lot, but the group has helped me. I have really come out. And I speak more now than I did. I'm not as uptight as I was.

"Sometimes certain things will bring it back. But it gets farther away as time goes on. I also try to watch television programs on battered women. That helps me to know that I wasn't the only one. When I first started hearing about these other women I'd think, it sounds like they were married to the same guy I was.

"I never thought I'd end up in prison. I never did anything wrong before. But something happened. I'm still trying to understand why."

SILENT TIME: *An inmate relaxes outside on one of the prison benches. The fact that she is unescorted, along with the color of her blouse, indicates that she has either a medium- or a minimum-security status.*

MAY

May is twenty-three years old and has been at Marysville for a little more than six months. She started out in minimum security, but was quickly reclassified to honor status. As a youth, May was a constant runaway, and was eventually sent to a group home, but she had never been in trouble with the law. She left the group home when she was seventeen, found a job, and worked her way through the rest of high school.

After graduation, she married her high school sweetheart. While separated from her husband, she began using drugs. She and her sister-in-law were caught attempting to steal a pair of shoes from a local store. She is serving a three-year sentence for attempted robbery; she had originally received probation, but her husband reported her for violating her probation by smoking marijuana. She was then sent to Marysville.

"I decided I just didn't want to be married anymore, so we separated. He wanted to talk it over, but I didn't.

"I've changed a lot since I've been in here.

"We had a good marriage. We (have) been communicating, and I'm thinking about getting together and working things out when I get out of here.

"I come from a good family. They wanted me to go to church on Sunday, and all of that. I just didn't want to. They were right. It would be depressing (to see them). I really don't want them to see me here. I'd want to go home with them."

NANCY

Nancy started selling real estate at age twenty-two. By the time she was thirty, she was one of the primary developers in the northwestern county in which she had been born and raised.

Three years later, she consolidated all her holdings into the redevelopment of a downtown block featuring a hotel/restaurant she had purchased the previous year. Exactly two years after the project began, a fire broke out in the hotel kitchen shortly after closing time. The fire quickly spread to the adjoining businesses. By the time the fire department was able to get the blaze under control, the entire block had been destroyed. Miraculously, no one was killed or seriously injured.

Nancy and two codefendants were charged with arson and aggravated arson; all three were convicted. Nancy received the longest sentence.

"I feel like I'm the kind of person who is regressing in here. Other people come here and acquire a GED or an associate degree, they take parenting skills, and they try to learn how to interact with people, and they go through their substance abuse programs. Those people can go out and really feel like they've gained something in here.

"I feel like if I don't get out soon, I'll have lost all my business contacts and all of my skills in order to function as a productive member of society. I'm regressing. And that's scary for me. I'm very confident that if I left here tomorrow, I could find a job in property management, or as a business consultant, or something like that. But I'm not too sure what will be available down the road.

"It's just incarceration. It's just a lifeless and spiritless existence. I have a lot of family support, and I've received a lot of community support since I've been in here. And, I still have a lot of self-esteem.

"But it's a very lonely existence for me, because for the most part, the things I see and the things I witness around here, I want no part of. It's instilled in me to be that way, and I feel like somehow that it's helping me to preserve my sanity.

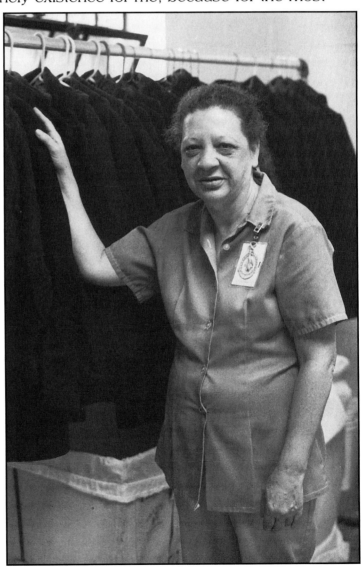

"I know a lot of the other inmates view me as uppity and snobbish and thinking that I'm better than other people, but I don't think that at all. I just know I come from a different culture and a different background. There's no common ground. So, why try to manufacture something that's nonexistent?

LAUNDRY ROOM:
This woman works as a laundry attendant for $18 per month.

"When I first came here, they tried to make trouble for me. They took my clothes out of the dryer and cut them up. I chose not to let that bother me, and I displayed no anger to give them the satisfaction that they really wanted to see.

"But I think now I've been here long enough to bear most people. Most people who know me respect me, and those that don't just leave me alone.

"I've developed a tongue since I've been here. Something I'm not proud of, but you have to in order to survive.

"When I lived in the dormitory for fourteen months, there were nights I just couldn't go to sleep because I was so afraid. Just my mere existence with these people, I didn't know what they would do. But I'm no longer living under that kind of fear. Once in awhile there's an encounter that makes me nervous or upset, but I try to use my vocabulary and my ability to speak on things rather than to have them pull me into their web of destruction.

"I think I've always gotten along well with the staff. I have good work scores. And I really try to do a good job, and I think they appreciate that. And I'm not a game player. I'm not trying to pass commissary and borrow and lend clothes and take things in and out of my workplace and all that kind of craziness that these women do. They're more concerned about their personal appearance and what they're going to wear tomorrow than how they're going to get out of here and what they're going to do with their life.

"I hope I can be even remotely the kind of person I once was when I get to leave here. It's a fear I live with. I fear I'll just wake up brain dead."

JUDY

Judy is twenty-five years old. This is her second time at Marysville. The first time she was in, she served nine months and received shock probation. She was a minimum-security inmate. This time around, she has a close-security classification.

"I come from an upper-middle class family, but I've always been different. I had very good role models, and I wasn't neglected. I'm just the one who got in trouble in school. I can't even say why.

"I got married when I was fifteen. My husband will be sixty-one this fall. We haven't lived together as man and wife for some time

"I was in an all black neighborhood. I was terrified. I was scared to death. Here comes this white guy in a pickup truck, and

I stuck my thumb out fast and he pulled over. I liked him because he smoked pot and owned a pool room."

LOIS

Lois is serving a three-to-ten year sentence for burglary and one year for probation violation. She has medium-security status.

"My drug of choice was marijuana. I've used it since I was thirteen. I've done everything. I mean, everything that's ever came out. My father was a drug dealer, one of the biggest in Dayton in my teenage years. So, drugs were always free to me and always available. When I got busted in '86, I'd been shooting up speed for like six years. But when AIDS came out, I put that down. And I stayed clean for about two years.

"I say clean, but I wasn't really clean, because I was still smoking pot. But I wouldn't touch chemicals. But then I got introduced to crack. And for about two months before I came in here, that's all I lived for. I mean, I didn't care about my kids. I didn't care about nothing but smoking crack. It was bad. Real bad.

"I was breaking in houses to get more crack. I was married for twelve years, a housewife. I turned to prostitution. I turned to the streets, lying, stealing. And It took me down real quick.

"My husband's mostly an alcoholic, but I did get him to smokin' crack with me there at the end.

BORED STIFF: *This inmate illustrates how time can pass slowly in prison.*

I had no discipline in my life at all. I was never told where to go or what to do. I was put out of the house at fifteen: told that I was old enough to do it on my own, that they couldn't afford me no more."

SHIRLEY

Shirley is a fifty-seven-year-old woman who looks much older. A minimum-security inmate, she is a few months away from the end of a five-year sentence for breaking and entering.

EXERCISE TIME: *Inmates in the highest maximum-security classification must spend their exercise time inside an individual exercise yard cordoned off by security fencing.*

"I'm five-foot five inches tall, and I weighed 101 pounds when I came in here. I'd been on a constant drunk for five years, and I was about two-thirds dead when I was arrested. I think that's why the judge sent me here—to save my life.

"I was living off of social security, but I had this bar tab and the bartender got it every month, except for the rent. I guess I was running up a tab anywhere between $250 and $350 a month. I kept getting drunk and I kept getting into trouble. This was the fourth time I was before the judge, and he asked me if he put me back on probation would I get in more trouble. And I said 'yes.' So, he sent me here.

"Five years, though. The two guys I was with? One guy got six months and the other guy got a year's probation. There are people who don't do this much time for murder.

"I got four grown children. Two of them live in St. Louis, and two of them live in Cincinnati. They don't know I'm in here. I've never let anyone know."

LEORA

Leora, forty-one, is four months into her third prison sentence. She has spent half her time in prison since age twenty-eight.

"I was an abused child. I was raped when I was a kid. But I finished high school, I had a job, a husband, and babies. I couldn't perform with my husband because of what had happened as a kid.

"Then I met a street man. And he made me feel good about myself because he wanted to use me. Finally, I saw something that was lower than me and that boosted me up on a higher class.

"I started writing checks to buy his love and his affection, and to buy things for my kids. I wanted to make everybody love me. Then, I found out you could buy affection with a checkbook. And it was something I was good at. And, it made people like me. And, I kept on until I wrote myself into prison.

"I was scared here. But I felt safe at the same time. I felt cared about. Most of my support came from officers. I lost my home and kids while I was here. Everything I worked for I had lost.

"When I left here, I didn't have a home. The only thing I had to wear was what I had on my back. And, I didn't know what to do. So, I went back to writing checks for my survival. And, I wrote myself back here again.

"I tried to pull myself together. At that point, I felt ashamed. I felt I let down all the people who tried to help me. I started counseling sessions. I was real depressed the second time around.

"The prison psychologist really helped. I fought it the whole time, but she stuck with me. I got paroled with the stipulation that I go through counseling, which I did. I stayed home four years which was good for me. I was working. I was content. I found Jesus, which I didn't here. I learned how to love God, and I learned how to love me.

GOOD DAYS: *This inmate is proud of the way she keeps her room.*

"But I was falling back into the same little box. I was writing checks, but I didn't get caught. Before I could get caught, a detainer came up from 1987, and I returned here. And, I know there's another one coming up. I want to get it over with here before I go out and start anew.

"I'm a good worker. But every time I'm doing good, I destroy it."

SANDRA

At twenty-seven, Sandra is serving her third prison sentence. First incarcerated when she was nineteen, she has spent more time behind bars over the past eight years than she has on the street.

Currently a medium-security inmate, Sandra has been at Marysville for a little over a year. During her second sentence, Sandra took part in the institution's now-defunct construction program. In that program, she learned all phases of home and commercial construction, and worked on rehabilitating homes near the prison.

"The first time I was in, I felt like I didn't belong here. My brother-in-law tricked us, and I got complicity to robbery. I felt like I'd been used. The second time, I was really hurting. My daughter was twenty-six days old when I came. I didn't get tickets, only two—compared to more than seventy the first time. I went to Lima and worked on houses. I could have used those skills, but I didn't. It didn't register. I just wanted to get back out there and jump into the same stuff.

"The third time, I felt s____. I felt I was a three-time loser. I went through a lot of self-pity, blaming others for my actions. I'm tired of coming here.

"I work on the yard crew. I keep the grass cut. I like the job because they put a lot of trust in you. I'm able to move about the grounds unsupervised.

"What I miss most, besides my family, is my freedom. It used to be they'd tell you when to take a shower. And I thought ain't that some s___? Everybody thinks people get raped and s___. Not here. I've never seen it in my three trips."

CLAUDIA

Claudia, thirty-two, is a medium-security inmate. She served ninety-one days at Marysville in 1988. A certified welder, she works in the prison garage, servicing state vehicles. Her brother is serving time in Marion, Ohio, and she often writes to him for advice.

"I swore I'd never come back here, but there's too many things to bring you back, you know? In a way, though, I guess I'm glad to be here. I was on drugs, and this place saved my life.

"I was on drugs a long time. My brother and my old man turned me on. Then, I met this guy. Man, I wanted him so bad I could taste it. He said I had to stop shooting up, or he'd leave. So I stopped, and we were together for four years.

"Then he got sent to prison, and I had to make do. So I started turning tricks to like get the car fixed or other things I needed. And when he got out, he didn't understand, so we broke up."

KATHY

Kathy has been at Marysville twice before. An admitted alcoholic and drug addict, she started using credit cards and selling the merchandise, as well as receiving stolen goods, to support her crack habit. Kathy's son, twenty-five and also a crack user, was her co-defendant. They are both currently serving time.

"I was a straight-A student in school. I got married when I was sixteen. My husband died when I was twenty-two, and I pretty much had an attitude after that. I started drinking a year or two after he died.

"The first drugs I ever took was crack. I got hooked on it the first hit. I'm not putting all the blame on him, but if it hadn't been for my boyfriend, I would never have tried crack. He said, 'I got something for you. Trust me. I'll never give you something that would hurt you.'

"Well, it hurt me. It hurt me bad. I have no idea where he is. He'll be around when I get out . . . like he was before, but I don't want nothing to do with him. I have no use for him.

"Maybe if I'd stayed away from this man, I wouldn't have been in any trouble, but we don't know that. He didn't hit me. He didn't break any bones.

"I started out as a pink shirt, but now I'm a blue shirt. I had some trouble with my roommate. And there was another incident where they found some pills on me."

CARLA

Carla, thirty-four, has spent exactly half of her life at Marysville. She is serving a life sentence plus seven to twenty-five for being an accessory to a robbery and murder. She is scheduled to appear before the parole board this year.

"I've completed my life sentence. I did fifteen years flat time, and that counts as life.

"There were four of us: my brother and another guy and two of us girls. There was no drugs or anything involved. It was just a robbery and a murder. The rest of them went into a bar. They were in the bar for about a half hour. I was just waiting outside. I had money to pay the cab driver.

"They hadn't planned nothing. Next thing I knew, a guy pulled a gun on the cab driver. Anita shot him in the head twice. My brother shot him in the arm. Jeffrey and I weren't there when it happened. We told them we wanted no part of it, and we got out of the cab and ran away before they shot them.

"My attorney messed me up all the way around. There was no plea bargaining or nothing."

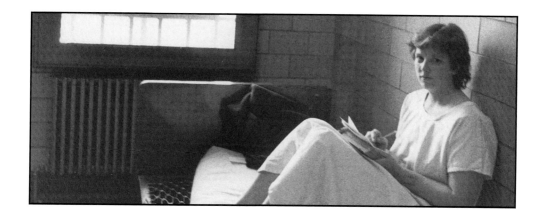

"It's just that you don't trust them."   2

T he staff at Marysville includes 147 female officers and 83 male officers. Men only can work in certain posts. For example, they may not work in any post that requires them to search inmates, and they are discouraged from placing themselves in any situation alone with an inmate. Men may work in the housing units, but only if a female officer is assigned there as well.

Because the facility is staffed by both women and men, personal modesty is strictly enforced. The inmates must remain covered at all times. They are not to undress in front of either female or male officers, and at night they must wear appropriate clothing. In the course of their sleep, should the blankets get kicked off and the clothing ride up, they could receive a conduct citation, commonly known as a "ticket."

As in many prisons, some officers remain a long time. Some come from families where several members work in corrections. The staff tend to view the inmates with a mixture of sympathy and distrust, and the line between staff and inmates always is drawn clearly.

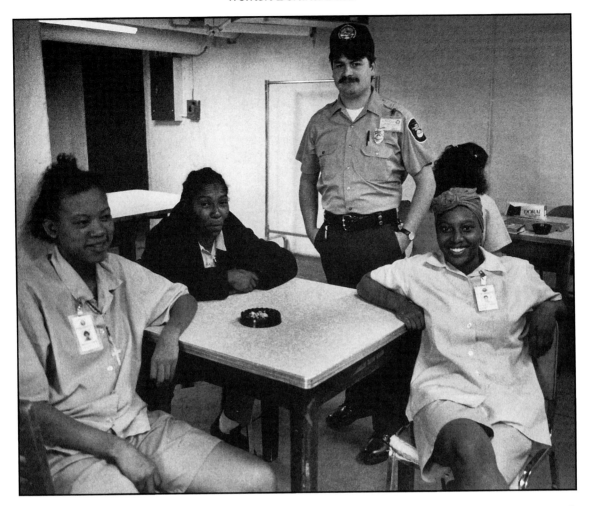

INMATES AND OFFICER. *The male officers have restrictions on where they can work and where they can work alone.*

OFFICER PAULINE LIGHTNER

Pauline Lightner has worked at Marysville for twelve years. She currently works in Reception, a busy area where all new inmates are processed.

"The women are allowed their basic underwear: bras, panties, socks. They can have their shoes (flat shoes), a tablet, pencils, pictures, cigarettes—if they smoke.

"They are not allowed hair dryers or curling irons. A lot of women like to have their jewelry, but they're not allowed to have much.

"What they try to get away with mostly are things like having their radio on after hours, or wearing their shorts too short. They won't have socks on when they are supposed to.

"I think there's a lot of stress for officers: I think officers have a lot of responsibility. There's stress that goes along with that. You have to account for their every move, and there's lots of stress connected with how the women are getting along, if there's arguments or someone is stealing.

"We have to be understanding of the inmates' problems, but they have to abide by the rules.

"The younger ones are more streetwise. A lot of them have no respect for rules and regulations. They can't follow orders. They have a tough time understanding rules.

"The older inmates are much easier to deal with. They give you very few problems."

OFFICER INEZ STARK

Inez Stark, twenty-six, has worked in several areas inside the institution. Her father, sister, husband, and brother-in-law also work in corrections.

"I don't think there's a whole lot of violence. You have a few who get violent. But as far as fighting . . . the women might yell and

YOUTHFUL INMATES. *With today's drug problems, an increasing number of younger inmates are being incarcerated.*

that . . . but as far as actually fighting, they don't do a lot of it.

"The majority of them want to do their time and go home. While they're here, they want to be with their friends. They don't want to go in the hole. They don't want to lose their visiting privileges.

"The ones who go to the hole are regulars. It's a fact of life with them.

"Being out of place is probably the most common infraction. There's drugs here, but I don't think it's as bad as the men's prison.

"I don't trust any of them. If I was in here, I would do anything and everything that would help me. There's always a motive for what they do. It's not that you don't like some of them. It's just that you don't trust them."

ELDERLY WOMAN IN CELL. *The officers maintain that the older prisoners present few problems.*

CLAIRE ADAMS

One of the senior administrators at Marysville, Claire Adams is an intense women in her mid-thirties with a no-nonsense approach and a reputation for getting things done.

"The women who are in here for killing their husbands tend to make ideal inmates. They never get a ticket (citation for misconduct). They go to church services, visit their families, and go to school. You see, they had a problem, and they eliminated their problem. Now they're getting on with their lives. Most of the older women are victims of abuse, but there are some younger ones. And it cuts across social strata. We have some very well-to-do women in here who have been seriously abused.

"It's been my experience that the career criminal will tend to stay in maximum security if they've been convicted of violent crimes. But the husband-killers will work their way down. I think most of these women want to get back on the right track. The recidivism rate for women is much lower than for men. It's less than 50 percent.

"One of the biggest complaints among the inmates is that they are treated like children. That's true. There's so much structure here . . . they're told where to go and when. But our job is to teach them the rules. They want to blame everyone else. But until you assume responsibility for your actions, you can't see anything wrong in what you did.

"(One) rule that's sometimes hard for outsiders to understand is our rule that the women keep themselves covered at all times. First of all, the rule protects the inmate and the officer. If she keeps herself covered, none of the male officers can ever say he was enticed or that she was making advances toward him. It also protects the officer from having a woman try to distract him or come on to him.

"It's definitely a bigger stigma for a woman to have been in prison than it is for a man. The public attitude is much harsher. I think the sentencing tends to be stricter. Personally, I think that 30 to 35 percent of these women don't belong here. A lot of them are just kids coming in for drugs. They need treatment, and they could be rehabilitated on the outside."

OFFICER CAROL LUTES

Officer Carol Lutes has worked at Marysville for more than ten years. During that time, she has seen the institution grow and its programs expand.

"I've seen women come in so-called normal, and I've seen them go downhill. Some women can do the time, and some can't. I'm a Christian woman, and I think if someone could only talk to them Christian-like, they could do the time easier.

"I've never had a problem. I go by the rules. I believe if you talk to them decently and humanly, you get that back, not all the time, of course, but most of the times that works.

"When I first came here, they were more confined. I find it less stressful now, even with more inmates. I've seen a lot of changes. When I came to work here, we didn't have any fences, no barbed wire. It was like a campus setting. They didn't put the fences in until about ten years ago. We kept getting more and more prisoners. But I think the neighbors were getting a little concerned, too."

OFFICER TOM FLETCHER

Officer Tom Fletcher has been at Marysville for five years. His father works at a men's prison in Lucasville, Ohio. He supervises the maintenance and repair of the institution's vehicles.

"The male staff are not to touch the women. It would have to be a matter of life and death before we could do that. The women officers can. And I cannot perform a search on an inmate. I would have to call a woman officer. Or a woman would have to physically escort her somewhere.

"I've never had an inmate approach me sexually. If I did, I would report her immediately. I had one; she was going back to her cottage and saying things were going on between us. I put a stop to that right away.

"I would not be alone with an inmate at any time. There are always two staff and four-to-eight inmates. The inmates might collaborate to falsify an accusation, but they would have to all get together. You never, ever go anywhere with just one inmate. Have at least two, and preferably three or four at all times.

"We had some problems in here a while back with male officers. Some of them got caught in the act, and some of them were reported by the women they were fooling around with. I definitely believe the women initiated it. But it's the officer's responsibility to know how to handle it. The staff knows that it's wrong, and they should never put themselves in a position where something like that could happen.

"I deal with murderers, sexual deviants, drug users . . . just everything. I've had a mixture of all of them. I don't trust any of them. I've got the first inmate who ever worked for me still working here. If I had to put my faith in anyone to protect me, I'd choose her, but I still wouldn't trust her with anything important to me.

"The best advice I can give to a new inmate is to be honest with yourself. Don't try to play games on the staff, and keep your eye on the other inmates. Some of them have been here three, six, seven times, and they know how to take advantage of other people. The biggest thing is to obey the rules.

"I haven't had any trouble with sabotage. I check everything they do. I have to train them. Start with the simplest things and let them work their way up. I have one minimum, up to max. They work together. The max people are usually the most discipline problems because they're not concerned about going to the (disciplinary hearing) board. They don't have much to look forward to.

"All of our tools are on a board. There's an outline of the tool drawn on the board. The board is checked before they leave. If everything is there, then they can leave. We watch the tools real close.

"I think they're getting younger. We have more crackheads, women burned out on drugs. I think eventually we're going to see more gang-involved. They're getting rougher and more prone to be violent."

INMATES ON OFFICERS

NANCY

(Nancy was convicted of arson and aggrivated arson; see page 9)

"The male officers have access to our rooms. We're not supposed to expose ourselves in any way, and we are responsible for the situation. We can be on the toilet or in our rooms changing clothes, and if they walk in on us, it's always our fault, and we get written up for exposing ourselves. I don't want that to happen to me. I don't want that on my record. They convert all of that into women trying to be seductive.

"It bothers me not having privacy with a female roommate. I will ask my roommate to leave the room when I have to shower or do normal bodily functions. I will not subject myself to that kind of dehumanization."

CARLA

(Carla, thirty-four, has spent half her life at Marysville; see page 17)

"I was kinda bad when I first came. I used to get in trouble a lot. Nothing serious. Contraband sugar. I would just do stupid stuff, like be out of place. One time I pulled my pants down and told the CO to kiss my ass. Then, I pretended to kill myself. I slit my wrists so they would let me out of isolation.

"I got a ticket about two months ago because I caught a guard looking in my room while I was dressing. So, I cussed him out. I said, 'What the f___ are you doing looking in my peephole when I'm dressing?'

"So he got me locked up. And when I was called to the captain's office, they didn't want to believe me. Now, why wouldn't he look. I'm a woman . . . he's a man . . . why wouldn't he look?

"I have a cyst in my back. This CO put his foot in my back. He thought I had some marijuana, which I did. But, it was never proven that it was mine. He kicked me in the back trying to get me to spit it out. And I had a cyst there for ten years. And my back hurt constantly.

"You check my record. I used to have a terrible temper. But now, whatever happens, happens. Sometimes I think they [the officers] want me out of here because I been here so long and I know everything that's going on."

CLAUDIA

(Claudia is a certified welder who works in the prison garage; see page 16)

"The CO's are kind of a mixed bag. There are some that's as good as gold, but there's some . . . this one guy . . . if you just look at him, you get a ticket for sexual advances.

"I don't like having male officers in here. I got a ticket once for disrespecting an officer. He walked into my room when I had my blouse off. He didn't announce himself or nothing. I think they either shouldn't be allowed in there, or they should announce themselves."

ANNE

Thirty-year-old Anne is a maximum-security inmate serving eight to twenty-five years for involuntary manslaughter. She has been at Marysville for four years. Anne stands five-seven and her hair is cut short and she has a full, thick moustache; she wears trousers and a loose-fitting blouse.

"As far as the male officers, a lot of the women around here are flirtatious. Now, if they see you undressed, they're going to look. They're men. They can write you up, but a lot of them don't. They give you a verbal warning. 'Cause they like to look.

"You can cover your peep hole when you're changing and there's a man on duty. But you just can't keep it covered all day. The toilet doesn't present a problem because it's in the corner and you can't see it from outside.

"The women COs can watch you shower, but the men can't.

"A lot of things can happen in the shower area. Especially when there's just a man on duty. There's also a woman on duty, but there's showers on both first and second floor, so she can't watch both of them at the same time.

"If an officer just pays attention to one of the women, she'll think he likes her. We got an officer in our cottage now. He's just a gentleman. He don't mean no harm. He's not out to hit on the girls. But just the way he talks, women think he be coming on to them. But he's an all right man."

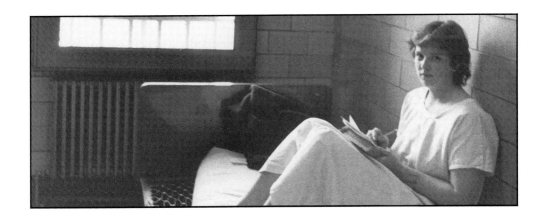

"Everything you hear, you've heard before." 3

Inmates at Marysville spend their time in very predictable ways. They work, they attend classes, they recreate. Any activity serves a vital purpose: to keep time from standing still.

Yet, there is more to prison life than simply keeping busy. The constant surveillance, the fact that one is never really alone, the monotonous routine, and the strict rules all create stress. Some find coping skills through their religion. Some simply learn the system and make it work for them. Some try to improve their lives and their future chances through self-help programs and schooling. A few shut themselves off from the rest of the reformatory whenever they can.

Food, of course, is a big part of an inmate's life at Marysville, and many of the inmates state flatly that the only meals they eat are prepared using food brought from the commissary. Part of the problem lies in the fact that the kitchen was originally built to handle 600 inmates, and it now handles almost three times that number. Another problem is constant turnover of inmate workers; efforts are being made to place more long-term inmates in food service positions.

"If these women could cook," smiles one female officer, "they probably wouldn't be in here."

Basic health care is provided through the reformatory's clinic. The medical staffing includes two full-time and one part-time physician positions, twenty-three nurses, a full-time dentist, and two part-time physician's assistants. The institution also contracts with a podiatrist, a gynecologist, and an ophthalmologist for weekly visits. Inmates are referred to the Corrections Medical Center in Columbus for more specialized treatment; surgery and advanced care cases are referred to the Ohio State University Medical Center. All medical costs are paid by the state.

COMMON AREA. *The women in a close-security cottage congregate in the common area to play cards, chat with their friends, or play games.*

Each year, about 10 percent of inmates enter the prison pregnant. This dictates special care and consideration, not only for their incarceration, but in terms of the anguish many mothers have as a result of "giving up" their babies only hours after they are born. Most pregnant inmates are transferred immediately to the Franklin Pre-Release Center in Columbus; those who are judged to be security risks stay at Marysville. The babies are placed with relatives or in foster homes a few days after birth.

The more crowded the facility becomes, the more precious privacy and individuality become. Most of the women share a room with at least one other inmate, and the inmates are always watched. Inmates and staff must wear identification badges at all

"Everything you hear, you've heard before."

EXPECTING. *Pregnant women are transferred to the Franklin Pre-Release Center in Columbus. Their babies will be taken from them within a few days after they are born.*

times. Six counts occur between four in the morning and midnight; during count, the inmates are to be on their beds. Every inmate should be accounted for at every moment, day and night.

To the extent possible, relations between the inmates are governed by facility rules. Inmates are not allowed to borrow from each other or sell items to each other. Fingernails must not extend beyond the end of the finger to prevent scratching. Inmates are not allowed to touch each other. Smoking can occur only in designated areas.

The rules of conduct include such infractions as fighting, using drugs, being disrespectful to an officer, and possessing weapons—which can include pens, lipsticks, or any other object from which a weapon could be made. Many of the rules and regulations at Marysville are designed to prevent the inmates from preying on one another. The limitations on personal belongings, packages, and

MEDIUM-SECURITY CELL. *An inmate reads during a rare opportunity to be alone.*

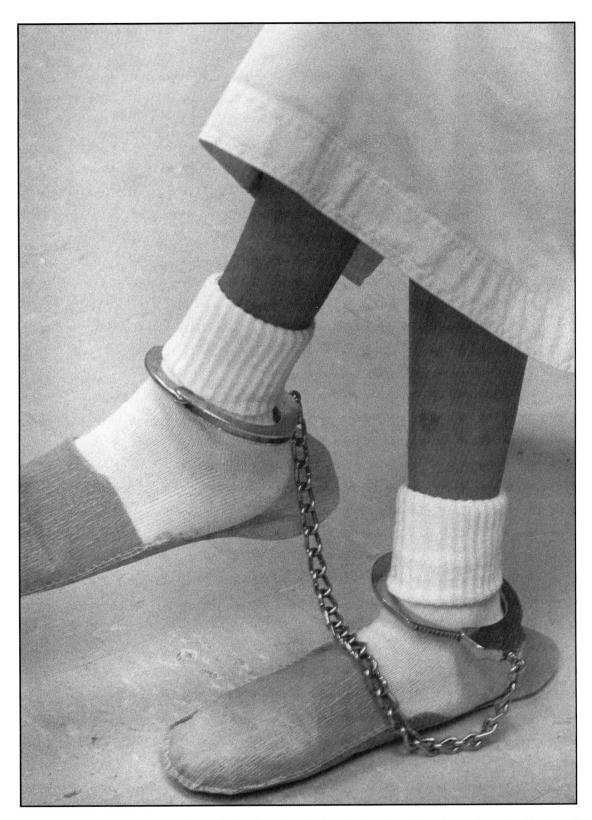

SHACKLED. *All inmates brought before the Rules Infraction Board are handcuffed and shackled.*

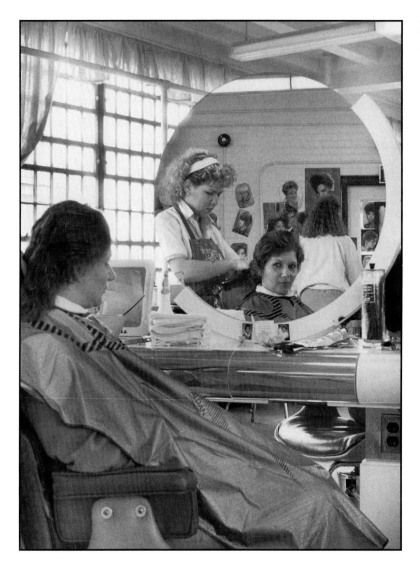

BEAUTY SALON. *Inmates can attend cosmetology school at the prison, and in turn, perform a service for the other women.*

bartering, for example, are implemented specifically to control an underground economy. The "no touching" rule helps to keep physical abuse and homosexual activity from flourishing. Much forbidden conduct occurs anyway, and correctional officers must make constant "judgment calls" as to whether a situation is serious enough to deserve a reprimand. As one inmate put it, "You are, after all, living with criminals."

When an inmate receives a "ticket," or written conduct report, she is usually called before a hearing officer who may issue a verbal reprimand, recommend counseling, or deny certain privileges. More serious cases are sent to the Rules Infraction Board, composed of three staff members. If the infraction is serious enough, the offender may be sent to the Disciplinary Control Unit, or as the inmates call it, "the hole."

For many women, staying away from the illegal activities is easy. Even those who receive the minimum state pay and have no outside income testify that they have enough on which to get along. Others, regardless of their income, want increased commissary purchases or favors from those who work in the beauty shop or the laundry. In the world of a women's prison, however, intimidation is mostly verbal. Even homosexuality largely is based on exploitation of the need to be comforted and loved rather than physical aggression. Real violence is rare; conning is an everyday art.

Most of the women cherish their ability to wear personal clothes, a little jewelry, and some makeup. It softens the knowledge that they have nothing that is secret or unique, nothing that has not been reviewed, approved, listed, or searched.

Within this structure, trust is perhaps the rarest commodity of all.

NURSE ELIZABETH SPENZ

Nurse Elizabeth Spenz is one of two nurses assigned to Reception. A middle-aged woman who has spent much of her career working for the state in drug and alcohol rehabilitation, she was assigned to Marysville eleven months ago. One of her duties is to test the inmates for HIV.

"When they are admitted, they are given a lecture on the medical services and how to use them. That's repeated again at the unit. Everyone forty and over has to have a mammogram once a year. They can sign up to go to the GYN clinic or the nurse's clinic at any time.

"But we're not a well-equipped hospital. And I hate to think about the women who never complain.

"If they have any of the high-risk factors, prostitution, drug users, then we recommend the AIDS test. It's a voluntary test. If they test positive, they are mainstreamed into the population. Since I started here eleven months ago, 1 percent have tested positive. I'm sure the rumor mill among the inmates has it a lot higher, but it's really quite low—a lot lower than I had expected.

"When they come in addicted, they go cold turkey. Except when they are pregnant. When they're pregnant is not the time to go cold turkey. So, then, they get put on methadone. Actually, those that go cold turkey have mostly done so in the county jail. They're usually pretty well dried out by the time they come in here.

"Most of the crack users are big alcohol users. If you're real

DISCIPLINARY CONTROL. *This inmate has violated prison rules and is in an isolation cell, often called "the hole" by inmates.*

high and you have to get to sleep so you can go to work, the way you come down is booze. You have to use some kind of downer. So, most people that are anything are boozers. If you're shaking, Valium is good because it stops the shakes and the boss can't smell it. Most of these . . . they know what to use . . . I mean, they're a walking pharmacy.

"When they first come in, they're given a tetanus shot and a TB test, then a urinalysis, a pap test, GC culture. That's basically it, unless they have a specific thing. Then, when the test results come back, they see the doctor for a physical. That usually takes two weeks, three, something like that.

"There's a long waiting list for mammograms at Ohio State. There's a long list for dermatology at OSU. There's no equipment here, so it's done at the University. They've worked on OSU coming out with one of those van things. But the basic thing is money. 'Do more with less' seems to be the famous quotation these days.

"The thing with drug users, is there is this rule of thumb. Whatever the chronological age was when she started using drugs is about the emotional age she is now. So you have these twelve- and thirteen-year-olds inside of a thirty-five-year-old body.

"It's usually poverty that brings them back. You send these women out of here right back into their old environment. If you're going to stay dry, you have to live in a dry environment. Poverty brings them back here. Poverty is probably the reason they were here in the first place.

"The saddest thing I've ever experienced here is hearing women say that they are glad to be back, because life here is better for them than the streets."

LEORA

(Leora, forty-one, has spent half her life in prison since age twenty-eight; see page 14)

"There's no one here I can say is a close friend. I do my time by myself. Some women have good friends. But I've learned not to trust people. I need to learn how to judge people and trust people. I always trust the wrong people. So, I'm afraid to get involved.

"I work in admissions. The women are so scared. They're sweet and they're innocent. And three weeks later, you can't recognize them. It's a mixture of all kinds of people in here. Some want to change. Some get an attitude. Some just want to do their time.

"Younger ones don't care. They're just doing a year. To them, it's a game. They're having a good time. They're drug dealers. Now, they can say they're hard. They have no respect for authority. Kids now, they talk to their mothers—crazy. How can you expect them to respect people their own age? It's sad. Every day it's kids coming in here. You get someone thirty-five and over, they're ancient. It's Romper Room now . . . the beep bop, the bop . . . it's all over the place. It's Romper Room. And they're not just coming to prison. They've been in juvenile. They're going out (from) there and doing it again.

"There's fights, but not much. The tension isn't that high. Basically, here a fight might be to hit somebody. No weapons. You don't have to be afraid that somebody is going to stab you or anything.

"People here will use you up. You help them out, and they won't pay you back. They treat you like you're a sucker for helping them.

"If you know you got sixty days or six months, it's play time. They're going to steal this and steal that, and they're going home. Then, they're going to go home and have a million stories to tell

MAXIMUM-SECURITY INMATE. *This woman had a lifetime of abuse from both her parents and her spouse. Like many victims, she feels she has it better in prison than she did on the outside.*

their friends and their boyfriends. They'll be a big shot on the block about being in the penitentiary.

"But this is nothing to be proud of. Prison isn't the answer. The answer is before here."

RACHEL

Rachel is thirty-three years old. She has been at Marysville for two years and is serving three to life, plus three years for the use of a gun. This is her first time in prison, although she was sent to juvenile detention when she was younger.

"I've been a blue shirt since I hit the farm (the reformatory). I can't go to school because I'm too far from my parole date. I don't think that's right. I think they don't want you to have too much education, because then you'd be able to pull stuff on the officers.

"My brother sent me a box. The Coffee Mate had to be poured

out, and they had a random drug search. They thought I had cocaine. Now, what kind of intelligence is that? I'm no crackhead. I'm not in here for drugs. But I had to strip naked and give a urine sample. I've been strip searched at work, too.

"I'm going to say what I want to say. I'm doing eighteen-to-life. What are they going to do to me? I get tickets, but they're minor tickets."

DARLENE

Darlene, twenty-one, is the product of a middle-class family. She grew up in a small town and graduated from high school without experiencing any contact with the law. After high school, she fell in love with a married man twenty years her senior. The two of them, along with the man's sister, murdered his wife. Darlene is serving fifteen years to life.

"If I had a deep dark secret, there's not a woman in here I'd tell. It's best not to confide in people. I learned that the hard way, when I was in the county jail. I told this certain individual about my case, because I thought we were friends and I could trust her. Then we came here and we didn't get along very well. We'd say 'hi' to each other, and that sort of thing, but that's all. Then, we had this confrontation, and we stopped speaking to each other. The next thing I know, she was showing newspaper articles around about my case, and telling people about my case.

"There's kind of a pecking order in here. The inmates are especially hard on people who committed crimes involving children. They're not physically abusive toward them, but they'll abuse them verbally. 'Child killer, child molester.' They do it to me. 'Murderer.' Just to make you miserable.

"I'm still catching on. I don't know all the games, but I'm catching on. But I didn't come down here to be liked. I pretty much stay to myself."

LAVERNE

LaVerne devoted most of her life to raising her three sons, occasionally working as a cashier when the family needed money. At sixty-two, she has been in prison eight years.

"Before I came here, I thought I'd be chained to the wall. But when I got here, I was very happy with the surroundings. It's nice. Shrubbery. Birds, squirrels . . . skunks.

"I've made some good friends here. The women are nice. And there's very few arguments. I think sometimes it's harder for the people on the outside than it is on the inside. You've got state clothes, you have a bed, you have a roof over your head, but every once in a while, you miss the finer things in life. The food packages and the clothes packages mean a lot. It picks your spirits up."

MARIE

Marie, twenty-two, has just completed the first six months of a three-year sentence for forgery. This is her first time in prison.

"They give you a little pamphlet, but all the rules aren't in there. And there's these crazy, crazy rules. They give us these scarves. But you're not allowed to put them on your head or wear them on your coat. What are you supposed to do with them?

"You know, you're not allowed to be in front of anybody else's door, but I had a friend . . . I made a friend, you know . . . and I stopped at her door to tell her to get up, it was time to go eat. And I got in trouble for that. It didn't dawn on me. Naturally, she was asleep, and I opened her door and said, 'Hey, get up.'

"I'm in the worst cottage here. It's called Harmon, and it's just a dorm: just rows of bunk beds. I hate that dorm. I work third shift, first of all. And I can't sleep during the day. And I can't very well tell them all to shut up and to quit going on with their day, because I'm the only one who works third shift.

"Around here if you lay something down, you'd better (be) damn sure (to) keep your eye on it because it's not going to be there when you turn around. For people that don't have money on their books to buy a lot, that's hard. And I don't. I went to commissary just the other day and I had ten dollars on my books. I bought cigarettes. And I'll bet you I don't have a pack of cigarettes left because everybody . . . and I know they got cigarettes of their own . . . but everybody in here has that personality. Get what they can get. There's a couple people in here I can trust. But I know they're not going to pay me back. But I can't say 'no.'

"It's hard to keep out of fights. Take last night, for example. There was this movie on television called *Jailbird*. These women escaped from jail. Now, I wanted to see this movie, and we had taken a vote on it earlier. Well, these girls threw a fit. They wanted to see Cosby. Well, they watch Cosby every night at five o'clock. And nobody argues with them. We let them watch it. So I got mad. I said, 'This ain't fair. You girls watch Cosby every night, and I want to watch this movie, and so does everybody else.' So we did get to watch the movie.

"It's hard. Somebody in the group always has PMS. And then there's just some natural born b_____.

"Misery loves company. I never said that until I come here, but it's the truth. If somebody's miserable, they want you to be miserable. I just got my high school diploma. And I was so excited. I got back to the cottage and these women were like, 'so?' I got so irritated. They were making me feel bad instead of good. I was proud of myself for doing something positive for a change. It's been a long time since I did something positive.

"I am not coming back here. I'm going to stay with my dad. My dad's an alcoholic, so I don't know how that's going to go, because I'm an alcoholic. My dad lives in a little tiny town, so I don't know what I'll do for a job."

DENISE

Denise, thirty-five, has been at Marysville for a little over two years. A minimum-security inmate, she has been reclassified and is getting ready to move to the honor camp.

"The lack of privacy puts a lot of stress on people. The only place where you can have privacy is in the [shower] stall.

"It's like being in a hen house. Women can't live with women.

"I haven't seen that much violence. I only saw two fights. They were just cat fights, one on one, no weapons. It starts with an argument. It's always something stupid. Women fight over the stupidest things. They don't go to the hole over fighting. They go to the hole over loud mouthing.

"There are snitches. And it becomes an obsession with them. Nobody harms them, though.

"There's a big difference with the younger women coming in. You got your crack babies coming in. They got this 'I don't give a s____' attitude. They're geeked up all the time. Nine times out of ten, the drugs are still in their system. They're rude. They're very disruptive. There's a lot of theft from them. There's a lot of petty fighting. The ones who have been here awhile tend to avoid them until they calm down and adjust.

"The ones that have a short time, they've got this 'I don't give a f___' attitude. And it's like 'I'm only here for a minute, so f__ you.' And it's like 'Stay away from me.'

"Anybody that's doing a year or eighteen months, or even six months, their attitude don't change that much. They're usually right back here in no time.

"The best advice I could give a person sitting in admissions would be: If you don't have somebody here that you know, get with somebody, or sit back and observe for a while. Get the feel of the place first, but don't cling to a person or get close to one person right away because it's strange in here. If you become close friends with somebody, rumors get started that you're lovers.

"What I did, I sat back. I just observed. I didn't try to be popular. I didn't try to make friends. I didn't use anybody, and I didn't let anybody use me. They are very manipulative with women right out of admissions. And if you let them play their games, they're going to use you up.

"I sat back for six months and watched. I didn't get close to anybody. I had one friend, but we never got close. We'd sit around in the rec room and smoke cigarettes and play cards, but I didn't let anyone know me until I was ready.

"It really shocked me when I got here. The state doesn't do anything for us hardly. If you have a problem, it may take a while. I've been lucky. I haven't had any serious medical problems. But I've seen others . . . elderly . . . who have suffered.

"The big cure-all here is Tylenol. Tylenol cures everything. I think I've built up an immunity to Tylenol since I've been here. And it's not extra strength, it's just regular Tylenol."

ALICE

Alice, twenty-six, is serving a one-year sentence for aggravated trafficking and failure to comply with the police. She has been at Marysville for seven months and is classified as minimum security.

"Some of the rules make no sense at all. It should be common sense, but it's not. Some officers go strictly by the book. Disrespect for another inmate . . . how can you go to the hole for that?

"The male officers hit on the women all the time. Sometimes it's the women starting it, sometimes the men. I think it's mostly the women who start it.

"You come in here as a woman, 100 percent. But the minute you step in here, you get into these games because people want to belong rather than be individuals.

"People perceive me as being a homosexual because I wear pants all the time. Or my hair is short. I'm not. Don't want to be, never will be. I'm not with that. If you're not a homosexual, don't play the game. It'll get you in trouble."

CARLA

(Carla, thirty-four, has spent half her life at Marysville; see page 17)

"I seen a girl get her ear cut off with a razor blade. Little things like that, which was big to me then because I was scared. As I got older, things started to get better, and I got wiser and learned how to play the game.

"Everybody here don't like everybody for real, but you gotta get along. There's not as many fights as there used to be. Now, it's just mostly talk. Now, they don't want their good days taken away or get their shirts taken away.

"There were only a couple hundred women here when I first came in. Everyone knew each other. I was in a cottage with all lifers.

"You think about being raped and killed and stuff, but it's not really like that here.

"I work in food service. I get twenty-one dollars a month. Sometimes I help people with their legal stuff, and I get paid for that. I trade and stuff.

"It's hard to get by on what you earn. I don't want to use state soap. I want to use the best that's available. Even if I can't afford it, I want the best. I don't want some generic product. I'm just like that.

"I had a private room until I went to the hole. Now, I'm up on the dorm. And a lot of women are jealous of me. I'm the biggest tramp. I mess with all kinds of women. It's just jealousy, because I don't bother anybody.

"But they all want something. 'Can I have a cigarette?' No. 'Well, lifetime-doing b___, you ain't never going home.' You know. That used to hurt my feelings, but it don't bother me no more, 'cause I'm not a lifetime-doing b___ no more. I only got a seven to twenty-five left.

"Everything here is based on a friendship. If you're cool with the right people, you can get up to the hairdresser for four or five packs of cigarettes.

"If you need to see the doctor, you help out the inmates who work up there; buy them some commissary. I got a friend working with every department. I don't have to pay them. I do favors on the

PASSING TIME. *Knitting and crocheting can help pass the time.*

food line, just like with the older women. I know when they come in, they'll be hungry, and I give them more food."

JOYCE

Joyce, fifty-one, shot her husband during an argument and is serving ten to twenty-five years for manslaughter. She also is serving an additional three years for committing a crime with a gun. She is currently a close-security inmate.

"It's not that hard to get along in here. Most of the arguments are over petty stuff—people stealing your commissary or your personals, or wanting you to do something for them.

"A lot of the problems in here are due to lack of respect. They don't respect theirselves, so they don't respect you. Women are just naturally mouthy. I don't want to see another woman for a hundred years after I get out of here.

"On a typical day, I get up about seven-thirty, get dressed, go out in the common area and have a cup of coffee. When there are classes, I go to school in the morning. Then, after lunch I'll go back to my cottage and do some reading or crocheting. After dinner, I'll go to recreation or just relax.

"It's normally just like living out there, only you just don't get on the phone and you just don't go out the door anytime you want to, but it's really not any different.

"Sometimes it's nice to have some privacy. Like this afternoon, for example, my roommate will be gone, so I think I'll just go back to the cottage and read or watch TV by myself. Sometimes just standing in the shower helps shut out the rest of the world. But I grew up in a large family with nine brothers, and I've always been around children and grandkids and stuff like that."

NANCY

(Nancy was convicted of arson and aggravated arson; see page 9)

"It's generally monotonous. You get up, get dressed, go to work, work all day. You don't deviate any day. Same thing day after day after day. You can feel good or you can go in when everyone's PMSing.

"Before we go into the visiting room, we have to squat, and we have to cough. They look under your armpits, and they lift your breasts up. They lift up your hair, look in your mouth, have you squat frontwards, squat back. Then you go in to visit your family. And when you leave, you go through the same strip, squat, and cough procedure again.

"There are good days and there are bad days. But mostly it's monotonous. And after a while everything you hear, you've heard before."

OFFICER INEZ STARK

(Officer Inez Stark, twenty-six, has a father, sister, husband, and brother-in-law who work in corrections; see page 21)

"They are allowed so many boxes per year and so many items per box. For example, one pair of shoes, six panties, six socks, etc. If they are here a while, they can acquire a pretty good personal wardrobe. They are allowed to wear their civilian clothes after four o'clock, and the majority of them do. First of all, they only have so many state pants, shorts, and skirts, and the more they wear their own clothes the better condition they can keep their state clothes. And, I think it makes them feel better.

"They can buy nail polish, [and] foundation at commissary. They are not allowed to have eyeliner. Nothing that comes in a glass container. I don't know why they're not allowed to have eyeliner.

"They can have pictures in their rooms. They are not allowed to have big posters. That would be contraband, but pictures sent from home or taken here, they're allowed to have all of that.

"When an inmate goes into the visiting room, she writes down everything she has on by name brand. If she has a watch on, she describes it. When she comes back out, she must have all these things on. If she's missing something or has something extra, she's stopped.

"They're allowed to have a gold necklace, but it has to have a cross and it has to be approved by the chaplain. They are allowed a watch. They are allowed a pair of earrings per box, and they are not allowed to go over the earlobe, and an ID bracelet. They are allowed to have a ring.

"In the visiting room, keep your eyes out for drugs, jewelry, and money. You look for them passing under the table. You watch the kids. They'll use the kids to hide stuff in diapers or whatever.

"They are allowed a hug and a kiss at the beginning of their visit and at the end of their visit.

"The majority of them want to do their time and go home.

"A woman who exists on state pay can get by, even if she smokes. You'll hear them complain that they don't have enough money because they have to live off of state pay. I disagree with that. If they have $22 a month, you probably have to spend two dollars a month. A lot of them buy soap and shampoo and things that the state already provides."

CLAUDIA

(Claudia, thirty-two, works in the prison garage, servicing state vehicles; see page 16)

"During my first trip, I used to get into a lot of fights. That happens a lot when you engage in homosexual activity. The younger girls are taken advantage of a lot. They tend to get involved in that kind of activity with their eyes wide open. I think it's because they think they have to have someone to have any self-worth.

"But I don't do that anymore. I tend to keep to myself. But if you don't have much money coming in, you gotta do something. So you iron clothes for people. You sell your medications. You do what you have to do to survive.

"Most of the fights in here are over women. You see, a woman to woman relationship is more dangerous, because a woman knows what pleases another woman. A woman gets turned out, and then she will kill for it. There's some women in here don't want to get out because they don't want to leave their lovers.

"I'm doing it in here, but I'll go back to men when I get out.

"They don't pay you enough in here. In order to get by, you need to do things. People around here will steal the panties off your body if you're a hard enough sleeper. They'll steal anything that isn't nailed down."

SANDRA

(Sandra, twenty-seven, who was first incarcerated at nineteen, is now serving her third prison sentence; see page 15)

"The homosexuals will form family units. They have mothers, sisters, brothers. Whole family. It happens a lot. They just want to belong, I guess.

"The younger inmates cause more trouble, but it's the older inmates who are the biggest manipulators. There's a definite underground economy in here. They call you up to get your hair done, but you pay them. If you want extra clothing, you pay for it in cigarettes. There's loan sharking going on in here. You pay back two for one.

"The majority of the fights come over commissary. Then, they fight over their special friends. Most of the time it's just screaming and yelling, but every once in a while they come to blows.

"A lot of women here were prostitutes to support their little drug habits, and I thought a prostitute laid on her back, got screwed, and got up, got paid, and left. Oh, no. That's not all they did. They do all sorts of really weird things. For a while, my eyes would pop open, and I'd think, oh no, they didn't do things like that. No, people didn't do things like that. But then, after you hear them for a year or two, and they're all the same, you're not even shocked anymore.

"I really feel disassociated from people in here because I was never into drugs. I was not a street person. I've never even been drunk in my life. And these people talk about all the things they go out and do, and I'm like, huh? Like I was popping popcorn last night and these two girls were talking about getting drunk and how they acted and they looked at me and like, 'How did you act?' Well, I've never drunk.

"It's not hard to adjust to wearing a uniform, it's just that what little identity you have is tied up in those personal items you have. To me, my music tapes are very important, but I wouldn't get into a fight over them.

"I like wearing cosmetics and getting dressed up. I do it for me. It perks me up, and you need that around here.

"There really isn't a whole lot of individual things you can do here. You just have to hold your own ideals and morals. I mean, you can dress up, but you're still in here."

HARRIET

Harriet has been in and out of prisons for most of her thirty-nine years. Her first trip to Marysville was in 1977, when, in her words, it was much nicer. In 1986, while serving time in California, she was diagnosed as HIV positive. She has been at Marysville for the past three years and is three years away from her parole hearing.

"After I got out of California, I went back to Cincinnati. Then, my father died, and it sent me into a deep depression. I felt I was being punished, and I went back to the drugs. I smoked crack, and I shot heroin, and when I ended up here, they put me in the hospital for the first thirty days. And I felt like I was being punished for my illness all over again.

"It's gotten a lot better since then. The other women treat me with loving care. I think it's because of my attitude now. I think I'm serving a purpose. You see, I helped start this group. It's called Positive Living. And we inform people about AIDS.

"I go into these deep depressions a lot, but I see a psychiatrist once a week, and that helps. I'm also taking college classes, and that keeps me busy. I spend my spare time in my room. My room is my castle. I can get silent and be with myself."

BETTY

Betty was twenty-five when she came to Marysville. She was originally classified as close security. After a series of violations, she was reclassified as maximum, the status she now holds after more than two years inside the institution. She is serving fifteen years to life.

"I didn't like it when I came here. But they said I had to pay a price because I took someone's life. It's just like the streets. The only difference is you don't have street lights and cars. I would like to go home. This is kinda boring.

"It's hard to stay out of trouble in here. You have troublemakers. You have homosexuality in there. You have, well, ah, you have everything. You got drugs. You got prostitutes. You know, all them different things. That's how it is in the streets.

"Like for example, we had two girls—they were lovers—in our cottage. One girl tells the other girl to leave her alone. The other girl won't leave her alone, so she beats her up. The police slammed her against the wall and put the handcuffs on her because they say she was resisting. So, the CO says she got kicked in the nose and all this crazy stuff, you know?

"I'm not used to getting up, doing what people tell me to do, and when to wash my butt or go to sleep or what to wear. I'm not used to that. But I'm getting used to it, because that's the way it is.

"But I'm not going to beg. I don't care if I'm here till doomsday, you will not take my pride. I killed somebody and I robbed somebody. Two cases ran together. I understand all of that. I'm here already. I am paying for my crimes. The fifteen to life was my punishment. But I don't think that anybody who has fifteen or thirty to forty to life has to keep paying with all these rules. Each time you do something, you get punished for it. I don't think that's fair."

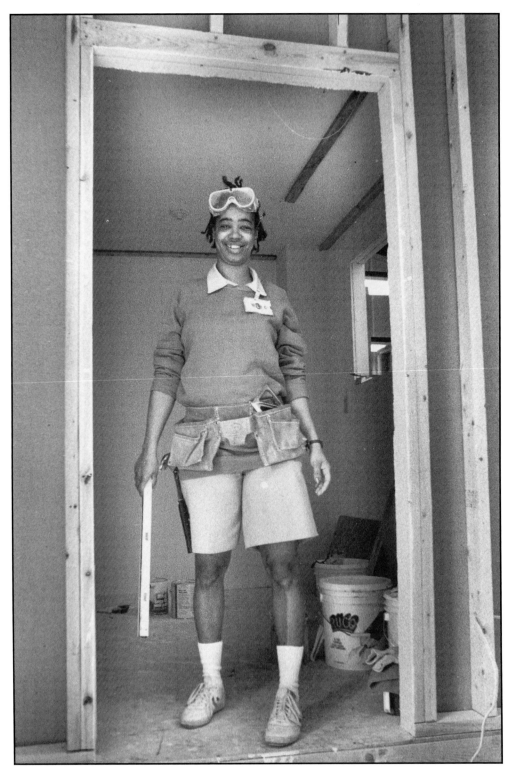

CONSTRUCTION CREW: *Inmates learn all phases of construction by building rooms then tearing them down again. For many years, the women of Marysville have rehabilitated homes in Lima, Ohio. Today, they go into the community and work on various civic and charity projects.*

ANNE

(Anne, thirty, is a maximum-security inmate serving twenty-five years for involuntary manslaughter; see page 27)

"If you want to get along in here, mind your own business. The women here don't know about friendship, about trust. You get close to someone and tell them all about your past. By the time you finish, they done added to it and subtracted from it, and it ain't nothing like you told them. And that causes trouble.

"That's how a lot of trouble gets started. It's best to just stay to yourself.

"I have a roommate. Close and max always have two to a room. You gotta have a job. The room's too small for both of you to be in there together very much. The best thing is to communicate with your roommate and set up different times to use it.

"I work in building trades. Being in max, I can't get good days, so getting every certificate I can get looks good when you go before the board.

"I want to show them that I have accomplished a lot since I've been here and I'm not involved in that negativity. When I first got here, I was rebellious and I had a problem with authority figures. I didn't understand people telling me when I could go outside and when I could walk in the yard.

"I didn't understand none of that. So, when I first got here, I was always going to jail (disciplinary housing). I used to get eighty to ninety tickets a month. Now, I've only had ten tickets in the past two years.

"A lot of the problem was over my moustache. I came in here with a real thin moustache. They made me shave, and now I've got a real thick one.

"It was like everyone was out to get me because of the way I looked. They didn't know me. I felt like I was with strangers. They would pick at me, and I would try to get them back. They would say something crazy to me, and I would say something crazy back to them, and I'd end up in (disciplinary housing) for six months.

"One time they had me go through this attitude adjustment program. After I spent seven months in lockup, I had to get a grip, because all I was doing was getting in more and more trouble.

"Every time I go to reclass, they bring up something I did before instead of looking at what I've done lately. They feel I still have an attitude problem. And I don't appreciate not being recognized.

"They want to keep knocking me down. They don't want you to have no spirit.

"My facial hair is natural. My mom is Indian. And all the women have some facial hair. I'm not trying to be nobody's man or nobody's aggressor. I can't help the way I look. I'm not trying to be nobody's boy. I'm not trying to get all kinds of women.

"I was being made to shave. So, I shaved and it came back thick, and I was scared. Then, I wanted to shave it off. But I didn't want the man telling me I had to, so I refused. Then, I got a hold of my family and my attorney, and they put a stop to it. I had to go to OSU and show them that this was all natural.

"Now I don't shave because I don't have to.

"If I got out tomorrow, I'd probably shave. And then go to a doctor and have something done about it. But I don't want to keep shaving it, because it grows back thicker every time. And I have sensitive skin because I'm a woman and shaving burns my skin.

"The moustache causes me a lot of problem with the new women. They see the blue shirt and they think we're all murderers anyway. Then, they see me, and they go to nudging each other and pointing at me. It makes me uncomfortable.

"I see women coming through CFS—our central food place—with beards. And they don't do anything about it. But they've always got me jacked up someplace.

"There's gays in here, but there's stereotypes, too. A lot of them miss their man. They look at me, and I'm the man they left at home 'cause they're not gay for real. It's just a thing to go through here. They just lonely and they want to be with somebody, 'cause everybody's with somebody. So, everybody thinks that's the way to do your time.

"So they see me and I be the first one they want to get with 'cause I'm so close to the black male.

"I just keep my distance. They don't know nothing about me. They just want to be with someone, and I don't want to play those games.

"The officers know it's going to go on. They'll write you a conduct report if they catch you. But they can't stop it. It's not forced on anybody. They all agree to it.

"It's all about commissary. Whoever can buy me the most commissary can be my boyfriend.

"I get eighteen dollars a month. I don't know who can get by on that. Especially if they have a boyfriend or a girlfriend.

"I get a lot of help from my family and my gentleman friend. I'd never make it on state pay. You can buy eighteen packs of cigarettes, two of every kind of candy bar. Plus, you buy stuff for your meals.

"You get your hot water from the coffee pot and you boil stuff. You can buy cans of shrimp and packages of noodles.

SERVING TIME. *Many of the women do the same thing day after day.*

"I've taken parenting. I don't have children. But there's only so many programs I can get into because I'm a max. And there's only certain jobs I can have because I have to be escorted. So, I try to get all the certificates I can get so it looks good before the board.

"When they open my file, the first thing they're going to see is all that negativity because of the way I was when I first came in here. But I was in OPI. And I was in AA. And the attitude adjustment thing. There was something on current events. And they'll see all of that.

"These things have been beneficial. The AA really helped me because I did have an attitude problem, and I did a lot of self-evaluation.

"I could use the construction work when I get out. I like to work with my hands.

"We have a problem getting medication because they're under-staffed and you have to wait.

"Having my family visit helps a lot. I haven't seen my mom for about six months, but she's going through a divorce, and she's got a lot of things going on right now.

"Today I got a pretty card from my mom and a money order. That helps. To know that somebody cares.

"There's no unity here. These women won't stick together. That's why there's so much trouble. It's all about money. People will use you and your money and your commissary. And the aggressor will save her own money and use the fems' money."

GRETCHEN

Gretchen is serving five to twenty-five for armed robbery. She is a close-custody inmate. At thirty-one, she has been at Marysville nine years. Her current work assignment is as a mechanic in the facility garage.

"I'm a blue shirt, and they don't have enough guards to escort us. I'm not involved in any of the programs. Sometimes you don't get enough time to eat. You just sit down and the officers say 'let's go.'

"When I first came here, everyone wore the same thing: red jumpers and white blouses. They started changing everything around in '87. Now, they put status with what you wear. They label-ing us when they put us in different shirts. They give pink shirts and green shirts a lot more privileges. And that ain't right.

"It's getting more and more difficult to live here because they keep coming up with more rules every day.

"I've had time added on to my sentence. I was in the hole from January 8 to March 15 for dealing in food boxes. A few years ago we had a sit down. I was one of them. But women won't stick together.

"There is a grievance procedure to lodge your complaints, but the staff sticks together and nobody never does nothing about it.

"I was gay since I was nine years old. I'd look at my friends and other women and stare at them. But if a guy touched me, I'd deck him. My momma took me to a hospital . . . a mental hospital . . . to find out what was wrong with me. The doctor told my momma I was gay. And my momma said, 'No, she can't be.'

"I was married to a woman in 1980. In 1990 she got killed. That's while I was in here. She got killed because she was gay. That hurts.

"I had one fight because of a relationship. Another girl came in and wanted to use her commissary to get to my friend, and I beat her up. I know it was wrong, but it ain't right to take advantage of someone because she's gay."

CLAIRE ADAMS

(Adams is one of the senior administrators at Marysville; see page 23)

"We don't have many of the problems that the men's prisons do. For example, we allow the women to have round-headed tweezers and scissors, and I know those would end up as weapons in a men's prison. The women can also check out razor blades. They have to return them when they're finished. But we simply don't have a big problem with weapons here.

"Now, don't misunderstand. We have some hardened criminals in here. And some of them have to be watched very closely. But we also have a lot of women who are in here for their first mistake.

"We have the rule here that says the inmates are not allowed to have any physical contact. No touching, no holding hands, no hugging, nothing. That seems hard for people to understand, but there are good reasons for it. For one, they could be passing contraband. Secondly, someone could be physically assaulting someone else. And finally, they could be physically stimulating each other. It's a security measure. With the rule in place, our officers can spot the possibility of a rule infraction immediately."

"If I know I have a visit..." 4

Although the female prison population in Ohio has been growing by leaps and bounds, incarcerated men still outnumber incarcerated women by an overwhelming ratio. Ohio has seventeen correctional institutions for men, located in nine different counties. When their classification allows it, every effort is made to house the men in the facility closest to their hometown. For female inmates, however, the logistics often work against the women being housed close to home. The state operates only three women's facilities, and two of them are prerelease centers, available only to women who are close to being released or who are pregnant. The overwhelming majority of female offenders are sent to Marysville.

That simple fact—which is repeated in nearly every state in the union—means that the families of female inmates often have to travel great distances to visit them. The physical distance and the subsequent economic hardship mean that for some inmates, a trip to the visiting room is a rare occurrence. (See *Parents in Prison: Addressing the Needs of Families* by James Boudouris, 1996, available from the American Correctional Association).

Physical punishment is nonexistent in this prison. What keeps the women on the straight and narrow day after day is the fear of losing some of their privileges. And contact with their families is generally regarded as their most valuable privilege.

VISITING HOURS. *Having a visitor can be a mixed blessing. The inmates are glad to see family and friends, but admit to missing them more after they leave.*

That contact comes in two primary forms: phone calls and visitation days. Minimum-security inmates are allowed unlimited phone calls. The women in medium security may make two calls per day, while the maximum-security inmates range from one call per day to four calls per week. Each inmate is allowed visitors, but her classification determines who can be put on the list and how many visits are allowed.

For many of the women, visiting day means being reunited with their children. An estimated 80 percent of the women left minor children behind when they entered Marysville. Nationwide, there are 56,000 children under the age of eighteen who have mothers in prison.

The visiting area is a single room with tables and chairs. It also has the potential for being the least secure area of the prison. Although the inmates are strip searched before and after each visit and the visitors themselves go through metal detectors, this is the area where the likelihood of contraband or drugs being passed is the highest. It is also a crowded room, and the officers have their hands full keeping an eye on everyone, including the children.

MOTHER AND CHILDREN. *Approximately 80 percent of the women in Marysville have children under the age of twenty-one who are on the outside.*

DENISE

(Denise, thirty-five, is a minimum-security inmate who has been reclassified and is moving to the honor camp; see page 41)

"I have a fifteen-year-old daughter, a twelve-year-old son, and a ten-year-old daughter. They're with my sister-in-law right now, and she has three of her own, so it's pretty rough.

"They live in the country. My kids were raised in the city. Their personalities clash. She's had them for a little over a year, but after school is out, the kids may go with their father or to a foster home.

"They feel very abandoned, very let down. After my husband and I divorced, I was both mom and dad for ten years. Then, all of a sudden mom has to go away.

"I've seen them once since I've been here. There's transportation problems, there's financial problems. I talk to them on the phone maybe once a month if I'm lucky—if their phone bill is caught up to where they can receive my call.

WORK DETAIL. *This inmate has completed her work assignment to clean the cottage showers.*

"I write them, I send them envelopes so they can write me back, I address them and everything, and I'm lucky if I hear from them once or twice a month.

"It's probably because they're kids. Probably because of the adjustment they've had to go through. Plus, they're in school, and they don't have much time. They live way back on a gravel road at the end of a lane. They have to walk almost a mile just to get to the school bus.

"I'm making excuses here. Because I'm sure if they really wanted to, they could write me more. But I go through my spells where I don't feel like writing.

"Excuse my French, but same s____, different day. Same thing happens day in and day out. Sometimes you just get into the rut of prison life. There's nothing happening, so why write."

LINDA

Linda is serving a life sentence; she has been at Marysville for the past eight years and is six years away from her first parole hearing. Linda lost her four children when she was sentenced, and she has not had any contact with them since. She does not know where they are.

"Someone sent me a picture of them last Christmas, and I'll be everlasting grateful for that. They've changed drastically, of course.

"I don't know if I'm allowed to contact them when I get out. Hopefully, they will contact me. I don't want to disrupt their lives, but I do want to get to know them again. The loss of children hurts worse than anything. Not just if you lose custody, but if you're separated.

"My best friend here has two children, and every time her children come to see her, she comes back from the visit in tears. She says it's so hard to see them walk out the door. So maybe it's (not seeing my children) a blessing in disguise.

"My friend's hearing of everything she's missing. At least I'm not hearing all that. I'm sure my kids are going through all kinds of things too, but I don't know what I'm missing. I don't think it's as hard on me as it is on her.

"Most of the time I don't think about it, because I can't handle it.

"I see a lot of people sit and cry and can't concentrate on their work after they've had a visit. They'll just be out of it because little Susie at home has gotten in some trouble, or when the kids are sick. That's a big thing, but you have to shut that off because you can't do anything. You just can't do anything.

"My dad's dying right now. I got a letter from my sister, and she said he probably wouldn't last another two weeks. Well, I can't deal with that right now. I got too many things to deal with in here. So, I just have to deal with that later."

JUDY

(Judy, twenty-five, has a close-security classification. She is at Marysville for the second time; see page 11)

"I have two daughters. Seven and eight. My mother and father are taking care them. My mom has legal custody. I don't have any plans to take them back. It would be unfair to them. The best I can do is get my life together so that they can see their mother is no longer in jail."

HARRIET

(Harriet, thirty-nine, was diagnosed as HIV positive in 1986 and has been at Marysville for the past three years; see page 48)

"It was a lot nicer when I first came here. There wasn't any fence, and we could wear our own clothes. And there weren't as many women. Our visitors could bring us dinner, and we could go outside with our kids. And you could have visits every day.

"I got a seven-year-old son, and they brought him up here for the first time a few weeks ago. He was so scared, he peed (on) himself. My other son is fourteen. He ran away from home a week ago and nobody's heard from him."

CLAUDIA

(Claudia, thirty-two, works in the prison garage, servicing state vehicles; see page 16)

"I don't see my children because my mom doesn't know how to get here. She gets lost on these side roads. So, I don't get any visits. That's what makes my time harder. I call my children and I talk to them. My grandmother sends me biblical messages through the mail."

OFFICER JACK RICHARDSON

Officer Jack Richardson is a tall man with salt and pepper hair and a grey moustache. One of the senior officers in the institution, he has been employed at Marysville for the past twenty years.

"What really gets me is dear old Grandma. She brings in four or five kids. And maybe it's the third time the inmate's been in here. So, here's Grandma bringing the kids in, and this inmate is all lovey dovey. Then, you see her out with her girlfriend all lovey dovey, see. Here's Grandma who has to take care of the kids. And believe me, that happens. Yeah, that's hard to watch. You know damn good and well that inmate don't care nothing about them kids or she'd be out there with them.

"Same thing with the husband. Here's a husband comes in and you know tonight she's going to have her girlfriend with her.

"Yeah, I feel sorry for the parents or the grandparents. They have to come in here year in and year out to see their daughter. It's kinda rough."

DARLENE

(Darlene is serving fifteen years to life. She and the married man she fell in love with murdered the man's wife; see page 39)

"If I know I have a visit two weeks from today, I know I'm going to stay out of trouble. It keeps you going. I go there happy and come back sad. I wish I could go with them, but I know I can't. Christmas is real hard. My birthday is three days before Christmas. Then, my Mom's birthday."

JANET

(Janet, late thirties, is a maximum-security inmate convicted of murdering her husband during an argument; see page 7)

"I was at County for six months, and they told me what it was like here, so I was ready to get here and start getting it over with so I could get back home to my children. I guess I was a little apprehensive when I first got here. I wasn't used to getting up at four-thirty or five to go to breakfast. And I wasn't prepared to be locked into a small room.

"It's gotten easier, now that I'm in population. I'm not so closed in. I spent three weeks in admissions, where you only get one ten-minute phone call per month.

"Now that I'm medium status, I can have a ten-minute phone call every day. I usually call my kids once a week on Saturday, then someone else in the family every Sunday.

"The kids are more relaxed now. But I don't know really. Their father isn't there anymore. And I'm not there. They are in counseling. It's hard. Especially with a teenager and a seventeen-year-old at that. I had the shock of my life the other day. He has long hair. And he wasn't allowed to have long hair. It took me three looks at him to recognize him. He's letting loose, I guess.

"If I can get out on super shock, he'd be nineteen. The next opportunity I'd have, he would be in his twenties. And if I serve my full sentence, he would be in his mid-forties. That's something to think about, isn't it?"

MAY

(May and her sister-in-law were caught attempting to steal a pair of shoes from a local store; she is serving a three-year sentence for attempted robbery; see page 9)

"I have two daughters, nine and three. The three-year-old always says she wants me to leave with them, and she starts crying. Being away from your children makes it difficult. Yesterday was my daughter's ninth birthday. I was really down. I felt like a failure.

"I always stress that it's not like the movies. I try to be open with them. Tell them why I'm here. When I was growing up, I didn't have this kind of honesty."

KATHY

(Kathy, an admitted alcoholic and drug addict, and her twenty-five year old son were both crack users and are both serving time; see page 16)

"I've hurt my parents. I'm the only child they've got. I've also got a young daughter that my parents are taking care of. Her daddy is serving life. It doesn't bother me when my family don't come. But when they come, I get depressed for a few days after they leave.

"A lot of these women abused their kids. Now, they'll tell you how much they loved them, but . . . there's this woman in my cottage, she kept her kids in the attic . . . left them for days. I didn't do that. My kids always had food. I was there when they were sick. There were times I wasn't there, but my mom and dad were."

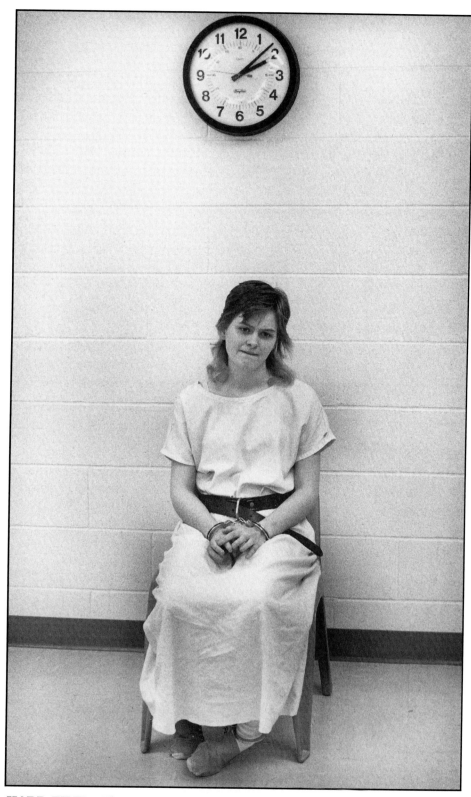

HARD TIME: *This woman is awaiting a hearing before the Rules Infraction Board. If convicted, she could be sentenced to Disciplinary Control and have many of her privileges taken away.*

CARLA

*(Carla, thirty-four, has spent exactly half of her life at Marysville;
see page 17)*

"My mother still visits. She's faithful. I got a good mother. And my sisters and my brothers visit. Well, my sisters don't come as much. And that's okay, because they got kids and stuff. And I think that's torture to bring the kids here. I mean, they don't know me anyway for real. And I had a brother born—I think he was like three months old when I came here—so he don't know me. He makes me feel uncomfortable. Plus, he asks a lot of questions.

"My mother caught a case (was prosecuted) twice because she wanted to see how they were treating me. She just missed me. So, she caught a case for shoplifting and got a six-month sentence. And she cried about it the whole time she was here.

"She used to sneak off and go to AA meetings and stuff, and I'd ask her why she was going behind my back, and she'd tell me she needed her good days so she could go home. And I'd say, 'Oh, you're a crybaby, momma. You came up here because you wanted to be with me, and now you want to go home.'

"But I got a good mother. We got to spend four months together. We got to spend Christmas together. It was really nice. First time in seventeen years."

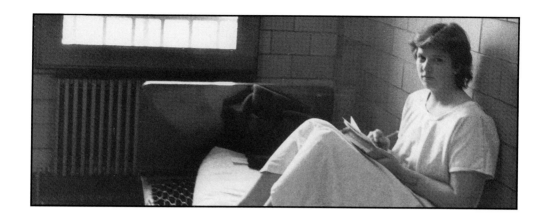

"You rehabilitate yourself." 5

In an effort to rehabilitate the women of Marysville, the institution offers a variety of educational services. All students who read below a sixth-grade level are required to take Adult Basic Literacy Education. Beyond that, there are the General Equivalency Degree (GED) and college programs, vocational certification programs, and prerelease classes. The institution maintains both a general and a law library.

The institution also offers substance abuse programs ranging from the familiar Alcoholics Anonymous and Twelve Steps to institutional programs like Tapestry and EMPOWER. Religious services are offered, and there are Bible study and fellowship programs available. The Family Services department of the reformatory offers classes in prevention of domestic violence and parenting skills. Recreational services at the reformatory range from softball and volleyball to weights to jogging.

OFFICER CAROL LUTES

(Officer Carol Lutes has been at Marysville for more than ten years; see page 23)

"I find it less stressful now, even with more inmates here. All we had for programs back then was cosmetology, OPI (prison industries), and the laundry. Today, we have all kinds of programs.

CLASSROOM STUDIES. *These inmates are working toward their General Equivalency Diploma.*

But if they want to be rehabilitated, it's up to them. Some of them have gotten two or three degrees, and they still come back. I've seen some of them come back four and five times."

DARLENE

(Darlene is serving fifteen years to life. She and the married man she fell in love with murdered the man's wife; see page 39)

"I work in the optical lab. I'm making twenty-seven cents an hour. I went through training. It's a two-year program. I'd like to do it on the outside. I'm cutting lenses to fit a frame. My father sends me about twenty-five a month. I get by on it.

"I think it would be harder if I didn't have this job. I really like the job. When I'm not working, I try to keep myself busy reading. I write a lot of letters, and I'm getting into needle work. I go to the weight room twice a week, (and) aerobics three or four times a week. I did seven months in the county jail. You basically just sit. That's annoying.

"You rehabilitate yourself."

SANDRA

(Sandra, twenty-seven, who was first incarcerated at nineteen, is now serving her third prison sentence; see page 15)

"I work in OPI (prison industries). I sew flags. I've done that for six years now, and I know everything there is to know about flag sewing. And I will probably never need to know it again. But I like to sew. Every once in a while, we'll have a special flag order and you get to design it, and that's kinda neat. But day after day of sewing the same things gets monotonous. It pays well, though.

"I haven't met anyone here who has any high self-esteem. I think most people think they're no good. They feel they don't have anything to offer, so they go out and try to make themselves feel good. The vast majority have very low self-esteem.

"As a matter of fact, when I was locked up, I used to hear some of the women talking about the men they were involved with and how these men would beat them, and they would laugh about it

FLAG LADY: *The women here make American and special flags.*

CLOWNING AROUND. *This inmate asked to have her picture taken.*

like it was normal. And to have to go through some of the things they went through. They really do not know how they are supposed to be treated. And that's really sad.

"Most of the people I talk to it's, 'Oh, I'm getting out next month, and I'm going to go get drunk,' or 'I'm going to get high.' Or, 'I'm going to kick that man's a__ who got me in here.'"

FLORA

Flora, thirty, was eight-months pregnant when she came to Marysville, and she was sent to the Franklin Pre-Release Center. She had her baby girl on a Thursday, and the prison authorities picked her up on Saturday. She took a parenting class and went through the Twelve Step program at Franklin.

"My incarceration was the best thing that happened to me. The past three years was just drugs. I went through programs, but they didn't take. I was on crack. I did a lot of things I didn't want to do because I was an addict.

"I first got involved with crack at a party. I liked it. I just kept on liking it. In the beginning, it was okay because it was free. But then I was broke.

"I was sleeping with this man and that man and the next man and neglecting my children."

BETTY

(Betty, twenty-five, was classified as maximum security after a series of violations in her first two years in Marysville; see page 49)

"It seems like the unit is not moving me like I want to be moved (out of maximum custody). Because I've been good. I haven't laid down in a year. But you got to beg and plead just to get your status dropped, and I don't think that's fair. Because if you work hard and don't get tickets, I think they should make you what you should be, but they don't.

"In July, I'm going to reclass, and I don't know if I'll get it . . . but I don't understand why if I've worked hard. They say I don't get in enough programs or it is the drug abuse. That has nothing to do with it. I think it should be based on your attitude and how you've accomplished things for yourself.

"I went to reclass in January, and they left me the same. They said I was doing good, but still they're not moving me. I have no knowledge of why. It's because they want you to suffer. I don't think nobody should suffer.

"Each year it gets harder. I've been here two years, and this is my hardest year."

CARLA

(Carla, thirty-four, has spent exactly half of her life at Marysville; see page 17)

"I started straightening up about '79 or '80. I took my GED here. I didn't pass. I also took cosmetology, data processing, and secretarial science.

"When I was trying to be good, this psychiatrist started liking me. He took advantage of me. The institution called it rape.

"The young girls coming in ask me for advice a lot, because I been here so long, you know. I tell them to get busy in the law library. Try to be constructive with your sentence. There's gotta be a flaw or an error somewhere. Instead of trying to get a green shirt and all that, work on your case.

"It's also okay to participate in different activities. Sometimes you gotta kiss a little butt, you know."

KATHY

(Kathy, an admitted alcoholic and drug addict, and her 25-year -old son were both crack users and are both serving time; see page 16)

"The short sentences I had before didn't do much. I just had six-month sentences, and I didn't go to one program. This time I got my GED, and I'm ready to go to college. I've taken the parenting class, and I've gone through Twelve Steps. I've learned a lot this trip. I'm not coming back again."

ALICE

(Alice, twenty-six, has been at Marysville for seven months and is classified as minimum security; see page 42)

"Right now I have no tickets. I've done everything they've asked me to do. I attend school . . . college. I work. I do whatever I can do for other inmates. But it seems the more you do, the worse you become. Especially if you're a blue shirt.

"This is not a rehabilitation center. You rehabilitate yourself. You know what you have to do in order to better yourself. The system is really messed up.

GIFT SHOP: *This inmate works in the gift shop at the main gate. Crafts and paintings done by the inmates are sold to visitors to raise money for local charities.*

"Don't be a people person. Be your own person. Look inside yourself and ask yourself how you want to do your time. You need something to keep your mind from vaporizing.

"I'm a book person. I stay by myself. I trust me and my higher power. And that's it."

JOYCE

(Joyce, fifty-one, shot her husband during an argument and is serving ten to twenty-five years for manslaughter; see page 45)

"I'm going to school to get my GED. I don't know how long it will take me to complete it, but I've come a long way. I dropped out of school in the fifth grade. I was fifteen-years old and pregnant.

"But I'm going to make it. I enjoy going to school. You need that education if you want to do things. I've learned that I'm not real smart. I have plenty of common sense. I guess I've been self-taught and I got by, but with an education I think I would have done a lot of things differently throughout my life.

"The earliest I'll be eligible for parole is nine and three-quarter years. It doesn't seem like a long time, maybe because of the way I think. I feel that you're doing time no matter where you're at. And it's not where you're doing your time, it's what you do with your time that counts.

PROUD MOMENT: *This inmate just received her high school equivalency degree.*

"I've gone through the Twelve Step program, and I went through Genesis I (a class for those who have been physically or sexually abused). I can't say it for everyone, but this has been good. It's been good for me. It's given me an opportunity to do things that out there I might not have ever gotten to do.

"I wouldn't know what it was like to feel like I had anything for me. Outside, my life was constantly going, but it was always for somebody else. I've never had the time to do things for me that I've had in here.

"That's awful to say . . . that you come to prison to feel free, but that's what I feel like."

DENISE

(Denise, thirty-five, is a minimum-security inmate who has been reclassified and is moving to the honor camp; see page 41)

"I got involved in drugs because I was the kind of person who thought you only live once. I'd try anything. But I was hooked from day one. And I was in a constant state of denial.

"I'm really surprised at what I've been able to accomplish educationally since I've been here. I got my GED, and I'm now in my third quarter of college. I'm really proud of myself.

"I didn't think my brain could work any more from all the drugs I took. But I went through the drug program, I got a certificate in horticulture, I got my GED, and I went through a parenting class. I feel like when I leave here, I'm going to be somebody."

ABOUT THE AUTHORS

Raymond G. Wojda has been a public relations practitioner for the past twenty years. He has received marketing and advertising awards from the Public Relations Society of America, the American Marketing Association, and the National Council for the Advancement and Support of Education. His nonfiction work has appeared in *Ohio Magazine*, the *Louisville Courier-Journal Magazine*, and various newspapers around the country. He is the author of *Behind Bars* (published by ACA), and is an honors graduate of the University of Michigan.

Judy Rowse is a social worker for Hospice of Clinton County, Ohio. Her writings have appeared in various newspapers and magazines, including *Living Single* and the *Wilmington News Journal*. She taught courses in English and social work at the Lebanon Correctional Institution and Wilmington College. She holds a bachelor of arts degree in English from Ohio Northern University, and a master's degree in social work from Ohio State University.

Grace L. Wojda is a freelance photographer from Yuma, Arizona. She was a participating photographer in the Homeless in America project which earned her the Leica Medal of Excellence award for photojournalism. Her work on life in the Lebanon Correctional Institution for men toured several major cities and was chosen for a three-month exhibit at the Smithsonian in Washington, D.C. She was the sole photographer for the book *Behind Bars*, and her work has been featured in numerous textbooks. Her photographs have also been featured in the *New York Times*, ABC *World News Tonight*, and *The Oprah Winfrey Show*. She is an honors graduate of Treasure Valley Community College and has taken courses at Boise State University.

DATE DUE

DEC 1 5 2003			